Reflections

An exploration of self through colouring,

mindfulness and focus

Tracy Badau

First published in the United Kingdom in 2016 by Badau Ltd.

Volume copyright © Tracy Badau, 2016

The moral rights of the author have been asserted.

All right reserved. No part of this publication may be reproduced, stored in a retrieval system, or transmitted in any form or by any means, electronic, mechanical, photocopying, recording or otherwise, without the written permission of the copyright owner.

ISBN: 978-0-9935753-0-3

A CIP catalogue record for this book is available from the British Library.

Printed in the United Kingdom

Reflections

An exploration of self through colouring,

mindfulness and focus

De-stress, Relax, Enjoy!

Tracy Badau

INTRODUCTION

It was 14 years ago that I left the UK to head off travelling for what I thought would be for a year. I had just come out of my marriage and taken voluntary redundancy from the investment bank I was working for. I felt at the time it was a great opportunity to take a break and see some more of the world. Little did I know that I was in fact embarking on what would become a journey of self-discovery and wouldn't see me settling back in the UK for 12 years. I arrived in Australia and fell in love with the vastness and beauty of the landscape and open skies, along with the welcoming nature of everyone I met on my journey.

I realise now, that I'd set off in search of something more, something that would take away the underlying feeling of anxiety and sensitivity to life that I was carrying like baggage. I was searching for happiness and peace and thought I would find it in another country, another relationship or another job.

Taking myself away from everything I knew, my family and friends, meant that I was now alone and had no choice but to confront everything in me that was feeding my pain. It took me to the absolute depths of despair and back out again. I now know, that for growth to happen sometimes we have to go through hard times to arrive at a more positive place.

What relevance, you may be asking, does this have to do with a colouring book?

As I went through my journey I was drawn to numerous self-development courses and events, meditation practices, books, movies and alternative healers that all had a part to play in my growth. Although, all of these sources speak in their own way and attract different people to their teaching, they are in fact highlighting the same message: that change comes from within. I finally woke up to an understanding that no external source was ever going to give me the happiness that I was seeking; it was, in fact, already inside me. I knew then that if I continued to carry my baggage with me wherever I went, it would block that happiness. I made the conscious choice to set it down and leave it behind me. In fact, at the time I not only set it down I visualised it being blasted off into outer space!

Does that mean that I am constantly happy and at peace, never dropping back into 'my stuff' occasionally? No not at all, I think it's incredibly hard to remain balanced in today's world, with the pressures we face on a daily basis. I still have moments where I am taken off centre and I drop back in, but it's far less than it used to be, never as deep or for as long. I now have the toolkit to pull me quickly back out of it. My emotional roller coaster could be described as more of a children's ride as opposed to the extremes of emotion that I used to feel. I find myself observing my reaction to an event that would normally have taken me into a negative space or victim mode. I start asking myself if that's really how I need or want to feel, the answer comes back no, and then I shift my focus back into a more positive frame of mind. I can do that because I am present enough to be aware of when it's happening and have a choice about how I respond. I choose not to buy into the negative thoughts that my mind is creating in that moment.

The reason I put this book together was to impart some of the knowledge and techniques I have learned and now use. They have helped me disconnect from the negative patterns and beliefs that used to run my life. I wanted to help other people on their journey. You will connect with some techniques more than others and that is absolutely fine, just as we all prefer different flavours of ice cream. Some of you may only want to use this book for colouring and that is perfect as well. This book is for you to use however you are drawn to using it.

The idea of these exercises or the colouring itself, is to create focus in you, to bring you into the present moment and out of thoughts of the past or the future. You can then start disconnecting from the patterns that are unconsciously running your life. The more we can disconnect from our familiar reactions, the more those patterns start to disassociate and drop away.

Before you move on to the colouring patterns and mindfulness techniques, I wanted to cover what I've learned about how our patterns and beliefs are formed in the first place.

Our brain is made up of tiny nerve cells called neurons which have branches that connect to other neurons forming what is called a neural net. Wherever these connect, a thought or memory is stored. We build up our model of the world through our association with memories from past experiences. These thoughts and feelings may also be linked in the neural net with other memories, thoughts or feelings.

For example, we build our concept of love from many different past experiences. Some people may connect love to disappointment and when they think about love they might recall a memory of rejection, pain or even anger which is linked with a specific person and then connects back to love. Our brains do not know the difference between what we are perceiving currently in our surrounding environment and our past memories, as the same neural net is being fired. If we practise something over and over, those connections form a long-term relationship and become the patterns that run our lives. So the reality is that we are often responding to events from our reference points of past experiences.

If we can interrupt our patterns, we start to disconnect the long-term relationships formed with our past memories and the thoughts and feelings associated with those, so we can begin to create healthier associations. Our emotions are an indicator of what our thought patterns are doing at any given time and we can create strategies to shift ourselves out of the current pattern if it is not empowering. Mindfulness techniques and colouring help us to do just that.

Mindfulness is all about living in the moment and not thinking about the past, the future or events taking place somewhere else. It is being fully present in the here and now. When we face challenges in life, if we come from a point of mindfulness it allows us to calmly assess our options and decide on the best course of action, rather than being reactive to events.

As we practice mindfulness techniques we learn to pay attention to our experiences, rather than the opinions formed by our minds about those experiences. We allow things just to be without judgment.

I hope you get as much out of this book as I did from my journey.

De-stress, relax, enjoy!

Lots of love,
Tracy. x

I would like to say a big thank you to all the beautiful people who have provided love and support to me through my life.

Many thanks go as well to the illustrators who have contributed to this book:

Mariya Soyanova, Akshay K.K, Elshan Burbanov, Ștefania Bălăucă, Catherine Gray, Rumi Das, Cerys Turner, Ana Novakovic.

> *"We can never obtain peace in the outer world until we make peace with ourselves."*
>
> **Dalai Lama**

Negative thinking

Although we try and stay positive, it can be easy to slip into negative thinking patterns. Whether it's worrying about past experiences, current stresses or an event in the future. We have a hard time getting out of our own heads, as we worry, obsess and feel anxious about all the things that might go wrong and it can be incredibly exhausting for us.

Often we have so many thoughts going round in our head, we find it difficult to centre ourselves and focus. Our thinking is often just habitual, an automatic reaction to our life circumstances. Research has proven that the average person has around 60,000-70,000 thoughts a day and around 70 per cent of those thoughts are the same ones you had the day before. So, although we may believe we have new thoughts every day, we think like we have thought in the past and what passes for original fresh thinking is often just mechanical and highly conditioned. A thought is no more than an opinion about some aspect of life. The mind observes the world and generates opinions to try and make sense of what is happening and why. Our thoughts are not an issue until we attach to them and start believing they are actually fact. This can be a problem if those regular thoughts are pulling us down, making us feel disempowered or stopping us from taking action.

Clearing the clutter

In order to start clearing our heads of this clutter, it helps to spend a few moments each day writing down anything that comes into your head. Don't think about what is coming out it doesn't matter, it is not meant to make any sense. It is just a way of excavating the unwanted clutter, in order to clear our minds so we can focus and be more present in each moment, rather than getting lost in the incessant thoughts.

Set yourself a target of writing at least two or three pages each morning. Don't think about what you are writing, it can be anything, nothing is too silly or trivial. Nobody is going to read these pages except you. You may not even feel it necessary to read these pages back yourself, as they are just a way of clearing out the fog so you can think more clearly.

> *"Be the change you want to see in the world."*
>
> **Mahatma Gandhi**

Reducing everyday stress

Zoning out in front of the TV is often the only form of relaxation many of us get after a stressful day. Some may turn to alcohol, drugs, smoking or food etc. to help suppress any feelings of anxiety. As well as being detrimental to our health, they do little to reduce the damaging effects of stress. We need to activate the body's natural relaxation response in order to relieve stress effectively.

Finding time to fit a relaxation technique into your life can help to reduce everyday stress, boost your energy and mood, as well as bringing your nervous system back into balance. Mindfulness exercises help us to connect with the present moment and disconnect from our incessant thoughts and worries.In the present moment, the here and now, there is no worry, anxiety or stress, only peace. If you don't feel comfortable doing more formal meditation practices, informal mindfulness exercises can help as an alternative. Often, these exercises are simply a means of bringing awareness into our life, daily activities and interactions with other people.

Read through each exercise before you begin so you can relax completely as you take yourself through it and remove all distractions before commencing. It may help to record yourself speaking through each exercise so you can play it back. If you do this, take time to read through it slowly and add pauses after each focus point to give yourself time to complete the exercise as you are listening back to it. You might also like to work with a partner or friend to take each other through the exercises.

Breathing mindfulness

This exercise helps to bring awareness to your breath. We are not usually aware of our breathing as it is automatic.

Sit in a comfortable chair with your feet on the ground. Start to feel yourself relaxing and allow the chair to support your body. You can close your eyes or keep them open, whichever makes you feel more relaxed.

Breathe in through your nose and start focusing on your breath as you inhale and then exhale through your mouth. Just pay attention to it, you don't have to do anything else just observe your breath as your diaphragm expands as you inhale and relaxes when you exhale. If you notice thoughts coming in as you do this, that's okay, just notice them and allow them to pass through like clouds in the sky. Thoughts come in and thoughts go out with no attachment and then refocus on your breathing again.

When you are ready you can bring your awareness back into the room, stretch your body and open your eyes.

To start with, do this exercise for five minutes and you can build up from there.

Whenever you start to feel negative feelings related to any thoughts, focus your awareness for five minutes on your breathing, wherever you are. We can then create strategies to shift ourselves out of the current pattern.

> *"The mind is everything. What you think you become."*
>
> **Buddha**

External focus

A good way to start observing mindfully is to focus on an external object rather than your internal thoughts or feelings. We tend to be less judgmental of an object than we do about what's going on for us internally. The external object is useful as it acts as a point of reference to which the mind can easily be fixed.

Focused observation exercise

Choose an object for this exercise, it can be anything from a pen to a mug or flower, something that is easy to hold and not too heavy. Sit in a comfortable chair with your feet on the ground. Start to feel yourself relaxing and allow the chair to support your body.

Hold the object in your hands and start to focus on it, allowing your attention to be fully absorbed by the object. Just observe it without any judgement or labelling. Take your time, you may find you notice thoughts coming in as you do this, that's okay, just notice them and allow them to pass through. Thoughts come in and thoughts go out with no attachment and then each time refocus back on the object.

As you continue to focus on the object, allowing thoughts to pass through, you bring your mind into the peace of the present moment releasing thoughts of the past or future.

When you are ready you can bring your awareness back into the room, stretch your body and open your eyes.

To start with, do this exercise for five minutes and you can build up from there.

> *"Nothing has meaning except for the meaning you give it."*
>
> **T. Harv Eker**

Being present

Often we find ways to numb pain in our body or we distract ourselves from feeling any discomfort. The purpose of this exercise is to simply notice your body in the present moment, accepting any ease or discomfort that may be present.

Body scan

Sit in a comfortable chair with your feet on the ground. Start to feel yourself relaxing and allow the chair to support your body. Close your eyes as you continue to relax.

Bring your awareness to the chair supporting your back and legs and all the places that it connects with your body. Notice your hands as they rest against your body or are supported by the chair. How do your clothes feel against your skin? Notice any sounds inside or outside the room.

Move your attention to your feet, feel the floor beneath them and become conscious of any discomfort or tension there. There is no need to judge or change anything just be aware. When you are ready, move your awareness now from your feet to your lower legs and focus on any sensations that may be there.

Continue moving your awareness gradually up your body to each part noticing any new sensations as you do. Take your time, you may find you notice thoughts coming in as you do this, that's okay, just notice them and allow them to drift by. Thoughts come in and thoughts go out with no attachment and then each time refocus back on the part of the body that you had got to.

Once you reach the top of your head, you can move slowly back down your body again. Notice any new sensations that may have appeared until you bring your awareness back down to your feet again. When you are ready, focus your attention back into the room and the chair supporting you, stretch your body and open your eyes.

To start with, do this exercise for five minutes and you can build up from there.

> *"A thought is harmless unless we believe it. It's not our thoughts, but our attachment to our thoughts, that causes suffering. Attaching to a thought means believing that it's true, without inquiring. A belief is a thought that we've been attaching to, often for years."*
>
> **Byron Katie**

Real or imaginary

Visualisation is often used by athletes as part of their training to cultivate a competitive edge, focused mental awareness and a heightened sense of well-being and confidence. It is the process of creating a mental image or intent of what you want to happen or feel, and can create a relaxed feeling of calm and well-being. Our brain doesn't distinguish real from imaginary. Research shows that if a person completes a task and another simply visualises completing the same task, identical areas of the brain are stimulated in them both.

Visualisation 1 – Achieving your desired outcomes

Put on some calming music and settle into a comfy chair with your feet on the ground. Start to feel yourself relaxing and allow the chair to support your body. Close your eyes as you continue to relax.

Spend some time thinking about your day or something important you have to accomplish. Visualise yourself performing whatever you have to do really well and achieving the desired outcomes from the situation. How do you feel? What are you thinking? What sort of things are you doing or saying as you complete the task? How does it feel to have accomplished everything you set out to do? Replay this scene a number of times until you feel confident and happy that you will get those desired outcomes.

When you are ready, focus your attention back into the room and the chair supporting you, stretch your body and open your eyes.

You can repeat this exercise for as many tasks or challenges as you like.

"Is it possible that we're so conditioned to our daily lives, so conditioned to the way we create our lives, that we buy the idea that we have no control at all? We've been conditioned to believe that the external world is more real than the internal world. This new model of science says just the opposite. It says what's happening within us will create what's happening outside of us."

Dr Joseph Dispenza

Visualisation 2 – Your favourite place

Put on some calming music and settle into a comfy chair with your feet on the ground. Start to feel yourself relaxing and allow the chair to support your body. Close your eyes as you continue to relax and let any worries you have drift away.

Imagine a setting that you find most calming, whether it is by a waterfall, on a secluded beach, a forest, meadow, a lake or a favourite childhood spot. Picture it in full colour – what do you see, hear, smell, taste and feel? Take a walk slowly around the area, notice the smells and colours and the textures around you. Maybe you can hear birds singing or can smell pine trees, feel the sun on your skin or cool water on your bare feet, as you breathe in and taste the fresh clean air. Enjoy the feeling of deep relaxation that envelopes you as you slowly explore your restful place. Stay there for as long as you want just soaking in the peace and tranquillity, this is your space and your time to savour every moment.

Don't worry if sometimes you zone out or lose track of where you are, just take yourself back to your calming place each time and continue on.

When you are ready, bring your awareness back into the room and the chair supporting you, stretch your body and open your eyes.

You can repeat this exercise as often and for as long as you like.

> *"If you do what you've always done, you'll get what you've always gotten."*
>
> **Tony Robbins**

Visualisation 3 – Ocean tranquillity

Put on some calming music and settle into a comfy chair with your feet on the ground. Start to feel yourself relaxing and allow the chair to support your body. Close your eyes as you continue to relax and let any worries you have drift away.

Imagine yourself walking through a forest towards the ocean. You can hear the waves up ahead and smell the ocean spray. The sun is shining and you can feel the warmth of its rays on your skin and hear birds singing all around you. As you walk along the path, you come to the edge of the trees and the opening takes you out on to the beach where a brilliant aqua ocean lies ahead. You take off your shoes and feel the soft sand through your toes as you walk. The waves are crashing on the shore and as you move closer to the water you feel the mist from the ocean on your skin and the cool water washing over your feet, giving relief from the heat. As you stroll along the water's edge, your worries wash away and you feel calm and relaxed, enjoying the peace of this moment. You walk further up the beach and sit down on the dry sand as you continue to soak in the scene, feeling more peaceful and relaxed as your stresses melt away.

Stay there for as long as you want just soaking in the peace and tranquillity, this is your space and your time to savour every moment. Don't worry if sometimes you zone out or lose track of where you are, just take yourself back to your calming place each time and continue on.

When you are ready, bring your awareness back into the room and the chair supporting you, stretch your body and open your eyes.

You can repeat this exercise as often and for as long as you like.

> *"Love yourself first and everything else falls into line. You really have to love yourself to get anything done in this world."*
>
> **Lucille Ball**

Visualisation 4 – Cultivating your inner garden

Put on some calming music and settle into a comfy chair with your feet on the ground. Start to feel yourself relaxing and allow the chair to support your body. Close your eyes as you continue to relax and let any worries you have drift away.

Breathe in through your nose and start to focus on your breath as you inhale and then exhale through your mouth. Imagine yourself in your favourite spot in nature, whether that's by the ocean, in a summer meadow, mountaintop or maybe a woodland setting. Visualise a pathway in front of you and walking along it. Take your time as you absorb everything around you, the smells, the sounds, perhaps the sensation of the breeze or the warmth of the sun on your skin.

Eventually, the pathway leads to a clearing and there in front of you is a garden. This garden represents your inner world. It is however you imagine it to be, there is no right or wrong, it may be a walled garden or surrounded by a picket fence, it is perfect for you.

Take a walk around your garden and notice any plants or trees growing there. How does it look, are the plants healthy and thriving? Or have the weeds taken over and the plants in need of care and water? Go round your garden and start to take note of anything that you want to change. Pull out any weeds or plants that you feel are out of place and don't belong in your garden any more. Plant some new plants that represent something that you want in your life or may want to change. Maybe it's a plant representing a new relationship, a new job, more money or another experience you may want. Give your garden lots of water and plant food to help it grow.

Then sit for a while in your garden, relax and take everything in. Stay there for as long as you want just soaking in the peace and tranquillity. This is your space and your time to savour every moment and you can come to your garden any time you like and continue to nurture and care for it. Don't worry if sometimes you zone out or lose track of where you are, just take yourself back to your calming place each time and continue on.

When you are ready, bring your awareness back into the room and the chair supporting you, stretch your body and open your eyes.

You can repeat this exercise as often and for as long as you like.

> *"Whether you believe you can or believe you can't you're right."*
>
> **Henry Ford**

Changing negative beliefs

Beliefs are incredibly powerful and help us achieve success or ultimately block our progress through life and drag us down. Our mind interprets events around us and spends time analysing and forming opinions about situations. When the opinion our mind has created about something resonates with us, a belief is formed. Most of our beliefs are formed unconsciously, whether through watching an event, or our parents, teachers, siblings or peers and absorbing everything like sponges. If we listen often enough to people telling us that we are no good at something, are physically not perfect in some way or should become something different to who we truly are, we start to believe it. Even just one significant experience in life can set up a negative belief pattern. Our filters are set to hone in on further instances that validate that belief and it becomes our reality and often a self-fulfilling prophecy. Because this happens unconsciously, we don't have the awareness to stand back and scrutinise how we are evaluating life through these filters or negative beliefs, so everything we see, experience, think and feel is adjusted to fit our beliefs.

Everyone sees life through their own filters, so our internal map of the world outside of us is unique and not the same as another person. We could be standing in a room full of people, the majority of whom are saying wonderful things about us but if we have a negative belief about ourselves, we filter those people out and only focus in on the two people that may be negative towards us. This then serves to confirm what we believe to be true about ourselves. It is quite incredible how our brain works!

Have you ever experienced a time during a conversation with a number of friends, where you perceived something very differently from other people that were part of the group and may have been upset by something that was said? The chances are, your filters were connecting to a negative belief about yourself that then related that conversation to a past experience and fired off a reaction in you. So in reality, you are not reacting to the conversation in the present moment but to the brain connecting with a past experience and negative belief that you may not be aware of.

If we have created an internal map with beliefs that see positive opportunities everywhere, our filters won't then see challenges as obstacles. That is not what they would be conditioned to hone in on, as it wouldn't fit with our internal map and beliefs. If however, we have negative beliefs creating our internal map of the world, every challenge that comes along will trigger a reaction and send us into a downward spiral, as our filter would view it as an obstacle and the world was out to get us.

We are all attached emotionally to our internal maps as this, as far as we are concerned, is the way it is and can be no different, we don't know - what we don't know.

It is as if we have created a mask, or self-image, during our younger years, assisted by the input we received from our role models growing up, that we now wear and that is who we believe ourselves to be. Our masks will determine how we view the world, whether our lives will be a success or failure, happy or unhappy, and whether we feel satisfied or not. The mask becomes so familiar to us, it becomes who we believe ourselves to be, and makes us feel safe and secure. To take that mask off and let go of the limiting beliefs about ourselves can be incredibly scary. We literally don't know who we would be and how we would function effectively in the world without that mask.

Another issue can be that we are often surrounded by people who also have a need for us to continue wearing our mask because it is serving them or feeding into their own internal map in some way. If we were to take our mask off and change that would then bring up their 'stuff' for them and some people are simply not willing to do that or go there. They may prefer us to stay as we are, so they can remain in their own safe place. In that respect, we would need to make a choice as to whether continuing to wear our mask is the healthy option for either party, even if it means we have to let go of some people along the way.

As it can be scary to take off the mask and we often resist changing, sometimes we will fight to protect our beliefs and will alter the meaning of experiences to validate that our beliefs about ourselves are correct. This may entail attracting situations and people into our life that will confirm what we believe about ourselves and continue to make us feel secure that our view is the correct one. If someone challenges one of our strong beliefs, we may react by attacking their opinion or credibility in order to safeguard our belief. We have to remember that all of this is taking place on a subconscious level and we are not aware that this is happening. Our experiences then start to become self-fulfilling, we have a limiting self-belief, we attract an experience or person into our lives that confirms that belief and it continues to go round and round.

Think about it for a second, have you ever noticed how you attract a certain type of person into your life; it may be that your relationships always turn out the same way, a different person, a different face but the same result? That's because you are attracting those types of people into your life, your filters are honed to only notice and focus on those people who will validate the limiting belief you have about yourself. In this way, our limiting beliefs also block us from recognising when someone is being kind to us, if we believe people and life are out to get us. We react to the person who is being kind from the perspective of the limiting belief, and if we do that often enough, that person will eventually respond in a way that will validate what we believe. Until you become aware of this and shift the limiting beliefs to stop this, the perpetual cycle will continue.

Most beliefs we have taken on board, particularly as we grew up, simply don't serve us any more as adults. If we can now start to dismantle our limiting beliefs and begin to replace them with more empowering ones, we change our internal map, take off our mask and start to see the world through different filters. We can then start to create and attract a very different reality.

How do we know what our limiting beliefs are? We can start by taking a step back and looking at our lives to see what we have created for ourselves. If your life has been full of crisis and littered with bad relationships or habits, we can start to dissect the limiting beliefs in us that have been creating that. They have shaped everything that we do and often prevent us from seeing opportunities or have even discouraged us from trying at all. The quality of our life is always a reflection of the quality of our beliefs.

It is important to note that not all of our beliefs are limiting, we will have areas in our lives that have been successful and are underpinned by empowering beliefs.

Start to begin uncovering areas of your life where you feel limited, hopeless or fearful. Your limiting beliefs are hiding out in the areas where you are producing results that you don't want.

Ask yourself the following questions:

o What area of your life do you feel frustrated with? Why do you think that is? Why are the results you have produced so far not in alignment with what you really want to be, do or have?

o How have the relationships throughout your life worked out for you? Have you noticed any patterns emerging?

o What area of your life have you really tried to improve but, no matter what, things just haven't got any better?

o What sorts of things don't you like doing and why is that?

o Are there areas of your life that you avoid, whether that's helping others or doing something that you have always wanted to do? What stops you or holds you back?

Anything that we say to ourselves to justify why things aren't working out is usually a limiting belief and it is getting in the way of what you truly want.

Some examples of limiting beliefs are:

I am not good enough, worthy enough, lovable enough, pretty enough, clever enough, successful enough, perfect enough.

We often say to ourselves on a daily basis statements like:

o I can't be my real self because I might get judged.

o I can't ask for what I want because I might get rejected.

o I can't fall in love because I'll get my heart broken.

o I can't trust people because I've been betrayed before.

o I can't do X because Y might happen.

o I can't pursue my dreams because I might fail.

o I can't be good enough because X happened.

Then ask yourself:

o What price in life are you paying for believing all of this?

o What impact does it have on you emotionally, physically or financially?

Write down all your limiting beliefs, acknowledging as you do that these are just beliefs, not the truth.

During this process, we may remember experiences from our childhood that were defining moments and where these limiting beliefs were set. If we can start to see the consequences and begin questioning the validity of our limiting beliefs, it will become clear that they are no longer serving us. It will then make it easier for us to begin disconnecting from them and moving towards more empowering beliefs. Some examples of empowering beliefs are:

o I am responsible for the life I create.

o I embrace challenges because I will always find a way to overcome them.

o I already have all I need to succeed within me.

o Every mistake is an opportunity to learn and grow.

o Setbacks are only temporary

o I can make tomorrow better than today.

Ask yourself:

What empowering belief would help me to succeed in this area of my life?

What are the different actions I can take to produce the results that I want?

What positive resources and beliefs do I already possess that I can apply to these areas of my life?

When we start to form more empowering beliefs, we begin viewing the world differently and life gets simpler and less chaotic. Start trying on different beliefs aligned with what you want.

Exercises for changing negative beliefs

1. Sit in a comfortable chair with your feet on the ground. Start to feel yourself relaxing and allow the chair to support your body. Close your eyes as you continue to relax.

Breathe in through your nose and start focusing on your breath as you inhale and then exhale through your mouth. Just pay attention to it, you don't have to do anything else - just observe your breath as your diaphragm expands as you inhale and relaxes when you exhale. As you focus on your breathing you will feel yourself relaxing more and more deeply.

When you are ready, think about all the negative beliefs that you have identified that no longer serve you. Imagine holding a deflated balloon in your hands and as you remember each limiting belief put the balloon to your lips and blow into the balloon as if you are releasing that negative belief inside the balloon.

Continue repeating this until you feel that you have blown all your negative beliefs into the balloon. Once you feel like you have let go of everything not serving you, tie the end of the balloon. Then picture or get a sense of yourself standing outside, it could be a favourite spot on the top of a hill or on the beach, wherever you feel happy and relaxed. Imagine holding the balloon at arm's length above your head and releasing it. Stand and watch as the wind carries the balloon away into the sky with all your negative beliefs inside it. Continue to watch as it disappears into the clouds and out of sight.

Then bringing your focus back into the room and the chair supporting you, turn you attention to all the empowering beliefs you identified, that would help you succeed in life. As you focus on each belief, take a deep breath in as if you are inhaling the belief into your body. Feel that belief being absorbed and integrated into every cell of your body and becoming part of you. Do this a number of times for each belief until you feel yourself filled with an array of empowering beliefs. Discover how it feels to stand tall, empowered and positive.

When you are ready, bring your awareness back into the room and the chair supporting you, stretch your body and open your eyes.

You can complete this exercise for as long and as frequently as feels comfortable to you.

2. If you have identified with a number of childhood memories or experiences that were defining moments where limiting beliefs were created, try the following exercise:

Sit in a comfortable chair with your feet on the ground. Start to feel yourself relaxing and allow the chair to support your body. Close your eyes and continue to relax.

Breathe in through your nose and start focusing on your breath as you inhale and then exhale through your mouth. Just pay attention to it, you don't have to do anything else. Just observe your breath as your diaphragm expands as you inhale and relaxes when you exhale. As you focus on your breathing you will feel yourself relaxing more and more deeply.

Imagine or get a sense of yourself sitting in a cosy room with a log fire burning in front of you. If you can't picture it that's okay, just get a sense or knowing that it is there. In your hands is a photo album containing pictures from your past. Start to turn the pages of the album taking those images in. If you come across a photo of an event that had a negative impact on your life and in turn created a limiting belief that you have identified, focus on that image for a second. Start to see the image in the photo fading and becoming more out of focus and continue to watch as the image gradually disappears altogether. When the photo is completely blank, remove it from the photo album and throw it into the fire in front of you as you release the limiting belief that was attached to that memory or experience. Continue moving through the album repeating the process for every photo that has a negative belief attached to it.

Start to imagine all the empowering beliefs that you have identified that you now want in your life. Imagine new photos of future events where you have those beliefs and are happy and successful. Take those photos and start pasting them into the new album of your life. Take a moment to turn each page and reflect on the new you and the new life you are now living. Feel how it feels to stand tall and feel empowered and positive. What sort of things are you doing, saying, hearing and feeling? Absorb everything that is going on in each of those new experiences.

When you are ready, bring your awareness back into the room and the chair supporting you, stretch your body and open your eyes.

You can complete this exercise for as long and frequently as you need.

Remember during this process to be kind to yourself Every time we criticise ourselves for taking the familiar path and buying back into a negative belief, we are once again strengthening the connection. Shift your focus back to the things that you want to do, on the positive things. Practise self-compassion and know that because you noticed yourself taking an old familiar path, you are now more aware of your actions and it is more likely that next time you will choose a new path. In fact, congratulate yourself for noticing your old pattern: awareness is half the battle.

"It is not the critic who counts; not the man who points out how the strong man stumbles, or where the doer of deeds could have done them better. The credit belongs to the man who is actually in the arena, whose face is marred by dust and sweat and blood; who strives valiantly; who errs, who comes short again and again, because there is no effort without error and shortcoming; but who does actually strive to do the deeds; who knows great enthusiasms, the great devotions; who spends himself in a worthy cause; who at the best knows in the end triumph of high achievement, and who at worst, if he fails, at least fails while daring greatly..."

Theodore Roosevelt

> *"There came a time when the risk to remain tight in the bud was more painful than the risk it took to blossom."*
>
> **Anaïs Nin**

Creating your future

Our 'timeline' is how we unconsciously store our memories or how we know the difference between a memory from the past and a projection into the future. Timeline techniques can be used to help free us from undesired negative emotions, limiting decisions and beliefs that prevent us achieving our full potential. We need to shed these so we can move forward to future goals and desires.

Having used the previous exercises to work on negative beliefs, the timeline example I've given here can be used to help create your future. A future derived from all the positive and empowering beliefs gained from the earlier exercises. The process involves using your imagination to create a compelling future that is inspirational and brings about your desired outcomes.

Timeline exercise

Sit in a comfortable chair with your feet on the ground. Start to feel yourself relaxing and allow the chair to support your body. Close your eyes as you continue to relax.

See yourself standing on the timeline of your life; see it stretching into the future in front of you and the past behind you. Begin by imagining all the empowering beliefs you now have from the earlier exercises, and feel how it feels to be that person standing tall and feeling empowered and positive. What sort of things are happening in your life now and in the future? Start imagining yourself already having achieved great success in all areas of your life. Keep playing that picture over and over to yourself and watch yourself move forward on your timeline through the rest of your life knowing that those empowering beliefs will always be with you. Repeat this process, of moving forward on the timeline through your life, a number of times to integrate the empowering beliefs and all the changes you are now seeing in your world.

You can complete this exercise as often and for as long as you like.

"When we are no longer able to change a situation, we are challenged to change ourselves."

Viktor Frankl

Afformations

These can be used instead of affirmations, which are short powerful statements aimed to create a shift in our minds. For example 'I am confident', 'Money comes to me effortlessly', 'I possess all the qualities needed to be extremely successful', 'I am healthy and happy'. These are used to keep the mind focused on a goal and are positive statements affirming that the state is already true with the hope of getting to that place. The issue with affirmations is that our mind will start to question them, our judgement kicks in and we hear our inner voice questioning the validity of our statement.

Afformations however, are empowering questions that we pose, instead of statements. 'Why am I so wealthy?', 'Why am I so confident?', 'Why am I so healthy and happy?' In asking the question we manage to sidestep our inner voice and instead the brain starts to search for an answer. We are literally giving our brain an instruction to look for an answer to the question and validate it. In doing this, we immediately initiate an action response as to how we are going to make it happen and change our subconscious thought patterns from negative to positive.

Write down a number of afformations relating to things that you would like to change in your life. Spend some time each day reading through your list, you can do this out loud if you want to, it's up to you.

"Promise me you'll always remember: You're braver than you believe, and stronger than you seem, and smarter than you think."

A. A. Milne

Human needs

It was during my Strategic Intervention course, with Robbins-Madanes Training that I learned about our Human needs.

Why do we do the things we do? We all have six fundamental needs that everyone has in common and we behave in certain ways to meet those six needs, often unconsciously.

We all have a need for the following:
Certainty: the need for stability, safety and comfort.
Uncertainty/Variety: the need for stimulus and change.
Significance: the need to be special and worthy of attention.
Connection/Love: the need to feel connected with someone or something. That you belong.
Growth: the need to learn and expand your abilities.
Contribution: the need to give to and support others.

The vehicles or behaviours we use to meet these needs are unlimited. When looking for certainty, in order to feel secure and comfortable, we may seek to control all aspects of our environment. To create a feeling of significance, we may tear others around us down or exercise power over them so we can feel more powerful and significant. All our needs are satisfied in either positive or negative ways.

If we are not consistently meeting our needs, we can often slip into dysfunctional behaviours as we feel out of control. When this happens people can fall into what is known as the 'crazy eight' pattern where we swing from one strong emotional response to another, as these responses continue to meet our needs. The two sides of the coin for the crazy eight pattern, are victim mode where we feel sad or depressed and use this as a way of connecting with ourselves. The other side is becoming frustrated and angry with life, often projecting this on to other people around us. We use this to feel a sense of significance and another vehicle for connecting with ourselves. As our body needs variety, we will swing from one side of the crazy eight to the other until we can get ourselves out of the pattern.

Often our issues start when we look for something outside of us to fulfil our needs, particularly our relationships. Unfortunately, nothing, whether it's the environment we are in, or the person we are with, has the ability to consistently meet our needs 24/7. Ultimately, everyone around us is also looking to meet their own needs in some way.

All of us strive for fulfilment in life in one form or another. If we focus on the last two human needs for growth and contribution, we are able to meet all of our needs in a positive way through our connection with other people. If we can shift our focus from looking outside of us to meet our needs and flip it in the opposite direction, to try viewing life from the inside out and what we have to give to other people or the environment, it will completely shift the way we meet our needs. It is the only thing that we can always be certain of and therefore is always a consistent way of meeting our needs, our ability to give.

When we give to another person, and it might be something as simple as a smile or a helping hand, we are meeting our need for love or connection with that person. We feel more significant and better about ourselves for doing it. Reaching out like this gives us variety in the respect we are connecting or socialising with lots of different people. It meets our need for certainty, knowing that we always have the ability to give - no matter how great or small.

Start to think about all the ways that you can share or give something to other people or to the environment. Think about doing this unconditionally, without expecting anything in return, so you are not giving to receive but purely giving something of yourself.

"Start where you are. Use what you have. Do what you can."

Arthur Ashe

Focus, meaning and physiology

The Emotional Triad, as it is called, is made up of your physiology, your focus and your language patterns which also account for our emotional experiences.

In order to feel a certain way, we adopt a specific physiology or posture (hold ourselves in a certain way), we focus on a specific thing (a past or future event) and use particular language patterns (our inner voice or self-talk). Often we are doing this to meet certain needs.

By changing our physiology, focus and self-talk when we are feeling down, we can shift ourselves out of the negative space we are currently in. For example, playing our favourite upbeat song and maybe even getting up and dancing to it, going for a brisk walk or doing some exercise. Regular exercise has the potential to ease symptoms of anxiety and depression.

You may also envision a time when you were in a happy space and feeling confident. Remember how you were holding yourself at the time, what your focus was on and the things you were saying to yourself and adopt that stance instead. When you make a conscious effort to smile and hold yourself more confidently, you fire pleasurable neural pathways in your brain.

Next time you are feeling down use one of these strategies to help you shift out of that negative space to a more positive frame of mind.

"The way our brain is wired, we only see what we believe is possible. We match patterns that already exist within ourselves through conditioning."

Candace Pert, PhD

Metaphors

We all think, speak and write in metaphors every day, without realising they are part of our language. A metaphor is stated as a figure of speech where an implied comparison is made between two different things that have something important in common. They carry meaning from one word, image or idea to another. Our brain responds powerfully to metaphors and it is important to understand that we also act in ways that are aligned with our metaphors. If we can start to transform our metaphors, we create transformation for ourselves.

If we think about the expressions we use on a daily basis to describe any challenges we may be facing, we can start to see the metaphors that play a fundamental part in our lives. Expressions such as 'I'm forever running up against a brick wall' or 'It's like talking to a brick wall', 'I can't see a light at the end of the tunnel', 'I think I'm cracking up', 'I feel like I've got the weight of the world on my shoulders'. These expressions are all metaphoric. We know there is no brick wall or tunnel but we register the nature of these expressions and accept them as embodying the experience, rather than being the experience itself. The walls and tunnels are representing the feelings we have of lack of progress, excessive responsibility, an unwanted state of mind and not having any hope. They are accurate descriptions of the depth and complexity of the situation. The way we think, make decisions and base our actions is on the metaphors we use; in this sense our metaphors determine how we live our lives and the kind of lives we live.

If we can start to transform our metaphors, we can shift our entire view of the world and open out to different possibilities and experiences.

Exercise for transforming metaphors

Take some time to write down some key metaphors that you identify yourself using on a regular basis. When you have completed this list, start to review ways that you can transform these metaphors into something positive and write this down. I have included some examples below.

o 'It feels like I'm dragging around a heavy rope'. To transform it, imagine taking a large pair of scissors or shears and slicing through the rope until it has been completely removed from you.

o 'I've reached boiling point'. To transform it, imagine standing under a refreshing waterfall soothing all your cares away and filling you with peace and calm.

o 'I've got a knot in my stomach'. To transform it, imagine taking the knot and starting to unravel it until it's completely undone.

Sit in a comfortable chair with your feet on the ground. Start to feel yourself relaxing and allow the chair to support your body. Close your eyes as you continue to relax.

Think about the metaphor that you want to change. For example, if the metaphor you are transforming was 'I feel like I have the weight of the world on my shoulders': picture yourself lifting the world, like a globe of the world, off your shoulders and setting it down by your feet. See how it feels to no longer be shouldering that weight and how free you now feel. What sort of things are you saying to yourself and to other people, what sort of things are you doing, now you are no longer carrying that weight and responsibility around with you? If you want to take it a step further, you could imagine blasting that globe in a rocket ship into outer space, as you won't be needing it any more.

If your metaphor is based on 'I can't see a light at the end of the tunnel', imagine yourself standing at the entrance to the tunnel looking in. Start picturing, or get a sense, of cracks appearing in the tunnel walls and at the end of the tunnel. Chinks of light start to appear, see those cracks beginning to grow as more light streams in. You may want to finish your visualisation with the whole tunnel collapsing and revealing a beautiful sky above, it is entirely up to you.

When you feel happy with how your metaphor has transformed, you can bring your awareness back into the room and the chair supporting you, stretch your body and you may open your eyes.

If a further transformation happened to your metaphor while you were completing this exercise, you might want to write down a description of how your metaphor now looks. When you are faced with a challenge that brings up an old metaphor, remember the new metaphor that you now have in your toolkit and move towards that instead.

Complete this exercise with as many of your metaphors that you want and as often as you like.

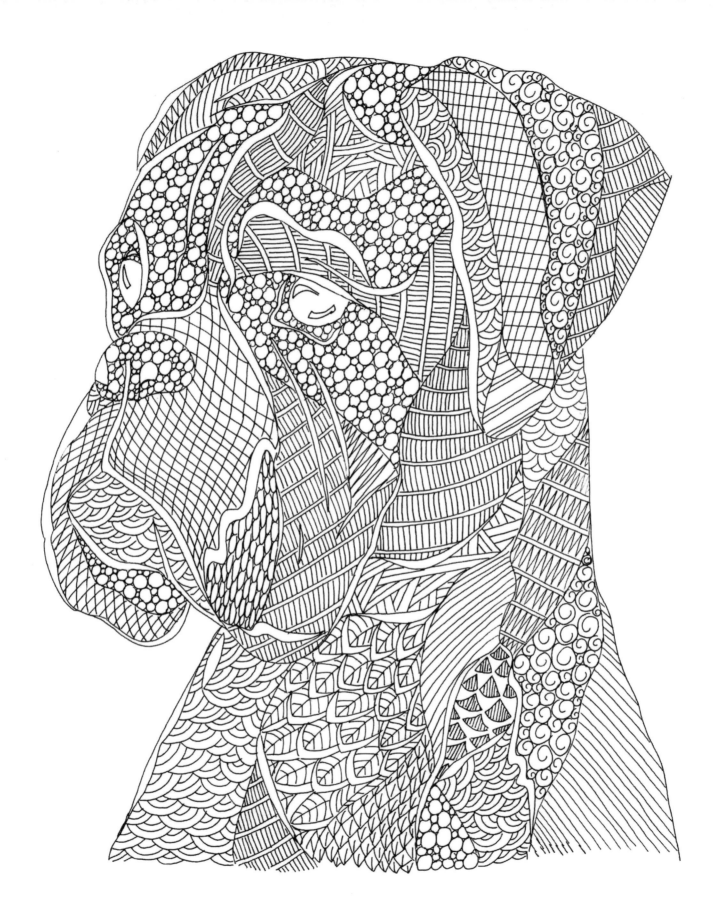

"Happiness is like a butterfly. The more you chase it, the more it eludes you. But if you turn your attention to other things, it comes and sits softly on your shoulder."

Henry David Thoreau

> *"None but ourselves can free our minds."*
>
> **Bob Marley**

Our attachment to thoughts

Often we treat our thoughts as if they were facts. We can always measure how positive or negative our thoughts are by the emotions we are feeling at any given time. Our emotions are triggered by us believing our thoughts. By understanding the way our thoughts and feelings interact, we can start to see through these conditioned patterns. Whenever we are feeling fearful, stressed, anxious or any other painful emotion; we have attached to a thought, even if we are not consciously aware of it. If we don't attach to our thoughts, then no negative emotion will arise.

When we accept things as they really are rather than perceiving them through our filters, or the opinions and judgments our mind has created, we start to see and live life very differently. When the mind is still we are able to experience the peace and joy that has always been there, it was just obscured by our mental chatter. We are then free from the worry and stress created by the future projections of our minds.

Question your thinking

As you start to observe your thoughts, ask yourself what buying into them does for you? Are they true? How do you react when you believe them to be true? Do they help? If the answer is no, then simply allow them to pass like clouds in the sky. Thoughts come in and thoughts go out with no attachment to them. Make it a habit to ask yourself, what is going on inside me at this moment? Focus your attention within. As we learn to disconnect our attachment to our thoughts, we no longer take the content of our mind as seriously. Our sense of identity does not depend on it.

"Believe in yourself and all that you are. Know that there is something inside you that is greater than any obstacle."

Christian D. Larson

Finding your inner resources

This exercise is great for tapping into your inner strengths when you need to. We often forget how resilient we are as people when life gets us down. Remembering a time when you did something really well, or when you experienced something amazing can help you to shift out of any negative thought pattern you may be in. You can then tap into that inner strength that is always with you, it hasn't gone anywhere, you've just forgotten about it.

Sit in a comfortable chair with your feet on the ground. Start to feel yourself relaxing and allow the chair to support your body. Close your eyes as you continue to relax.

Remember a time when you faced a challenge, got through it and came out stronger at the other end. What resources did you need to get you through that challenge? Did you need confidence, or the ability to speak up for yourself, was it great organisational skills or patience? When you came through the challenge, remember how you felt. How were you holding yourself? What sort of things were you saying to yourself? (inner talk). Were you congratulating yourself for a job well done - for getting through it? What were other people saying to you? Sit for a second and take in how amazing it felt, remembering that you can tap into those resources again at any time. Those are qualities that you still possess; you just have to remember that they are there!

When you are ready, bring your awareness back into the room and the chair supporting you. Stretch your body and open your eyes.

Complete this exercise for as long and frequently as you feel is beneficial.

> *"When one door closes, another opens, but we often look so long and regretfully upon the closed door that we do not see the one which has opened for us."*
>
> **Alexander Graham Bell**

Listening to our intuition

Often we find it hard with the stress of everyday living to quieten our minds enough to listen to our inner voice or we don't trust our intuition to follow its advice. Unfortunately however we are often very good at listening to our inner critic. The following exercise can help you to bring a more healthy perception and understanding to difficult situations. By imagining yourself asking the advice of someone you admire and respect the opinion of, you are actually circumnavigating your inner critic to tap into your own inner wisdom.

Listen to your inner coach

Think about someone that you admire, this person can be someone you know or don't know. It could be a positive role model that you have grown up with, a teacher or sports coach. What traits does this person have you admire that can be cultivated further in yourself?

Sit in a comfortable chair with your feet on the ground. Start to feel yourself relaxing and allowing the chair to support your body. Close your eyes as you continue to relax.

When you are relaxed, imagine the person that you admire sitting beside you and ask them for guidance. What would they do if they were you, how would they handle the difficult situation, what would they say and what action would they take? Now take a moment to listen to their response and the feedback they give to you. If you have any more questions that come up, ask them and once again listen to their response.

Continue with this until all your questions have been answered and you now have a renewed confidence to face your challenge.

When you are ready, bring your awareness back into the room and the chair supporting you. Stretch your body and open your eyes.

Complete this exercise for as long and frequently as you feel is beneficial.

> *"To love oneself is the beginning of a lifelong romance."*
>
> **Oscar Wilde**

Taking some time out for you

Our lives are often so busy that sometimes we forget to take time out and appreciate ourselves. Sometimes simply pausing and taking some time throughout the day to take a break can help. Stop what you are doing, look out of the window, take some deep breaths and allow your mind to calm down.

Make it a point at least once a week, more if you are able, to take time out for you, doing something that you enjoy. Anything that confirms that you are worth spending time with, something that is just for you. It's about putting yourself first to connect, nourish and nurture.

- Go for a walk in nature. Walking releases endorphins and helps you to switch off from any pressures as you take in the scenery around you and get into a steady rhythm.

- Have a warm bath. This can help your muscles to relax and encourages a general feeling of relaxation.

- Listen to some calming music.

- Have a relaxing massage.

- Read a book.

- Do some colouring.

- Take a Yoga, T'ai Chi or Pilates class as these are designed around relaxation and breathing techniques.

Often we feel that it is too hard to take time out as we have so many responsibilities and people relying on us. When we understand the benefits of taking time out, we realise that it is important for us. It enables us to then go on and support and give to others. Taking this time helps us to connect with ourselves and we come away feeling rejuvenated and revitalised. Nourishing your mind and body is the most basic form of loving yourself!

> *"Be not afraid of life. Believe that life is worth living and your belief will help create the fact."*
>
> **William James**

Mindfulness cues

It helps to have a few tricks up our sleeve as quick techniques for whenever negative thoughts and feelings begin to enter our heads. Mindfulness cues are reminders for us to return to the present moment and remove any distractions and the stress created. Establish a number of mindfulness cues that you can trigger to help pull yourself out of a downward spiral before it takes control.

- Focus your awareness on your breathing for five minutes, wherever you are. You may want to imagine that every time you breathe out you feel the stress leaving your body and as you breathe in you start to feel more calm and relaxed.

- Focus on your hands and clench them tightly for five seconds before releasing and opening the palms out. Repeat this for a few minutes.

- Listen to your favourite song and pay attention to how it makes you feel.

- Go for a walk in nature or if you are at work around the office.

- Choose one action that you can do every day mindfully. It might be when you make your cup of tea in the morning or brush your teeth. Make a conscious decision to be mindful while doing it.

- When you walk to work in the morning make it a habit to notice three things about your surroundings that you have never noticed before. This will keep you focused on the walk, instead of thinking about something that happened the day before, or worrying about something in the future.

- Break your patterns or routines. There are many things that we do the same way over and over again, day after day. These become automatic and present a great opportunity for the mind to wander. Bring more mindfulness to your day by breaking these routines. If you jog along the same route every day, try a different route or reverse the order in which you normally towel yourself off after a shower. When you break your patterns and routines it will force your mind to focus and pay attention.

"Create the highest, grandest vision possible for your life, because you become what you believe."

Oprah Winfrey

Self-compassion

We all feel compassion towards other people, but unfortunately we forget sometimes to feel compassion for ourselves.

Sit in a comfortable chair with your feet on the ground. Start to feel yourself relaxing and allow the chair to support your body. Close your eyes as you continue to relax.

Think about people in your life that you love and feel care and concern for. Imagine sending those people lots of love and happiness. As you do this, notice how good it feels when you connect with those feelings of compassion and loving kindness. Now direct it inwards. Imagine yourself standing in front of you and receiving that compassion from yourself. If it makes it easier, you can imagine yourself when you were younger. Allow your feelings of love and compassion to be directed towards the younger you; filling them with happiness, peace and love, and easing any suffering they may be going through. Give the younger you a big hug, knowing that you can come back and give yourself some love and compassion any time you want.

When you are ready, bring your awareness back into the room and the chair supporting you. Stretch your body and open your eyes.

Complete this exercise for as long and frequently as feels beneficial.

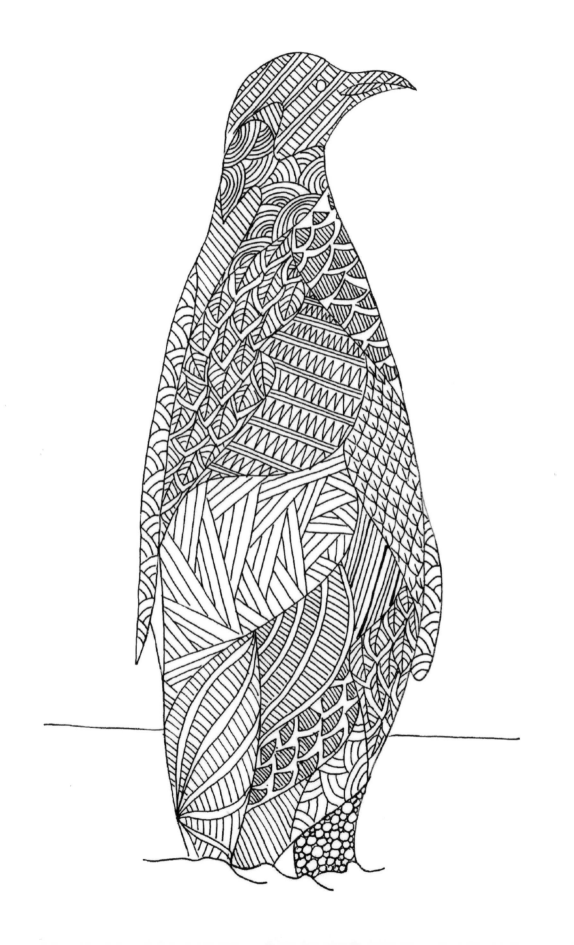

> *"It is not in the stars to hold our destiny but ourselves."*
> **William Shakespeare**

Circle of Excellence

The Circle of Excellence helps to recapture memories of doing something really well and connecting with the positive resources that we have inside us and sometimes forget. Using this technique we can gather powerful internal states from our unconscious and make them available whenever we need them. It is also a way to gain control of our emotional states which influence our behaviour and therefore the results we get in life.

Step 1

Do this exercise standing. Think about a context or situation that you would like to improve. What do you feel about that situation, what are you seeing, hearing and saying to yourself? Work out what intention you have to improve that area of your life. Imagine yourself drawing an imaginary circle around that context on the floor and set it to one side; we will come back to it later in the exercise.

Step 2

Now it's time to start setting up your Circle of Excellence, to work out the resourceful states that would be most effective in relation to the context of the situation you want to improve.

Create an imaginary circle on the floor. Stand outside the circle and recapture memories of doing something really well in the past, where you used positive resources that would be of benefit to the context you want to change. Step into your Circle of Excellence and imagine dropping those resources into the circle. Step back outside and shake off your body as this helps to clear the state and return you back to neutral.

Remember another memory or resource that would be useful, step back into the circle and drop that resource into it. Step outside the circle and shake off your body every time to return your state back to neutral. You may also like to think of some additional resources you can add to the circle, maybe you need some more confidence or organisational skills, the ability to speak up for yourself or some extra courage, any resource that will help you with the context you want to change.

After doing this a few times, drop the final resources into your circle and stand inside it for a few moments to feel the shift in state that all the combined resources are giving you. Step back outside your circle and shake off the state.

Step 3

We are now going to set an anchor for this state. An anchor is a stimulus that can be used to set an internal response by using an external trigger to access a desired state quickly. Think about an anchor that you want to use, make it an action that is not obvious to other people. It might be squeezing your forefinger and thumb together, pressing your palm against your thigh, touching your earlobe or scratching your chin, any action that you are comfortable with.

Step 4

When you are ready, step back inside your Circle of Excellence and feel the shift in state that your combined resources give you, as you do this fire off your anchor, for example squeeze your forefinger and thumb together if that is the anchor you have chosen. Do this a couple of times, stepping out of the circle each time and shaking off the state, just to make sure it is fully integrated.

Step 5

When you are ready you can fire off your anchor again without the need to step into your Circle of Excellence as you now have your anchor set. Check as you do this that your resourceful state comes back so you know that your anchor works. Once again shake off the state.

Step 6

Now come back to the original context that you put to one side and stand in front of this circle. Think back to that context you want to change and remember why you want to improve the situation. When you are ready, step inside the circle with the context in and fire off your anchor. As the new resourceful state takes hold, start to see how it transforms the original context, what is now happening in that situation, what are you seeing, hearing and feeling now you have additional resources to call on? Take in all the changes and appreciate how that situation now plays itself out.

Now remember that you can call on this resourceful state whenever you need it, in whatever context. You may want to create a number of resourceful states with your Circle of Excellence that you can use for different situations and set different anchors for. Use it in everyday life, before you go into a challenging situation just fire off your anchor.

It is always a good idea as well to revisit each resourceful state every few months as you may want to add some additional resources.

"The love that you search for everywhere is already present within you. It may be evoked by any number of people or events. But finally, you must realise that you are this love. The source of all love is within you."

Gangaji

"What lies behind us and what lies before us are tiny matters compared to what lies within us."

Ralph Waldo Emerson

Gratitude journal

Keeping a gratitude or appreciation journal is a way of remembering and celebrating the things you are grateful for in life, even the small things. In doing this it helps you to focus your attention away from any negative thoughts you may be having and on to more positive things. It is another way of interrupting our negative patterns.

Make it a rule that you are going to complete your journal every night before you go to bed and write down a list of 10 things that you are thankful for that day. It could be as small as being grateful for it being a lovely warm day or someone smiling at you on the train to work. We often forget the small things and focus only on the things that are not going so well for us in life. If you try and vary what you write down, it makes it more challenging and helps you to find new things to be grateful for that you may not have noticed.

You may start by writing down some of the basic material things you are grateful for in your life: your house, your clothes or the food you have to eat and maybe move on to the people you have in your life or the things you love to do. Turn it inwards and write down all the things you are grateful for in and about yourself.

This is your journal so you can write about anything that you appreciate. Start to think about what these things give or do for you and how they make you feel as you are writing them down.

"Realise deeply that the present moment is all you ever have. Make the Now the primary focus of your life."

Eckhart Tolle

Being present

In our minds the present moment hardly exists as we live in the past and the future most of the time. Even when we do focus on the present it may be through the eyes of the past or we reduce each moment to a means to an end to project us forward into the future. It really is the present moment that holds the key to our freedom, but as long as we are a slave to our minds, we cannot be present in each moment.

Our emotions are our body's reaction to our mind. Fear comes in many forms, as worry, anxiety, stress and unease and is always related to something that might happen, not something that is happening in the here and now. Have you ever worried about something in the future and when it finally arrives, it was nowhere near as scary as the image of it you had created in your mind? In fact, you sailed through it effortlessly. We can always cope with the present moment, but can't cope with something that is only a projection of the mind. The more we are able to honour and accept each moment, the more we free ourselves from pain and suffering.

If we remember back to when we were young children, we weren't in our heads, we were seeing and discovering the wonder of life, light, shapes, colours, textures, hearing noises, watching rain trickle down a windowpane, picking up golden leaves in the autumn. Start to use your senses fully again and take a look at what's going on around you, without interpretation or judgement, say yes to each moment. Get out of your mind and be fully present in order to see the beauty of life.

You can start to practise being present in your everyday life by taking a routine activity and giving it your full attention. When you do the washing-up for example, focus on every item that you are washing, the feeling of the water on your skin, the movement of your hands or the scent of the washing-up liquid.

> *"You cannot solve a problem with the same mind that created it."*
>
> **Albert Einstein**

Looking at a challenge or situation from a different perspective

Sometimes we are so close to an issue that we lose perspective and can't see the wood for the trees. We become so rooted with concerns at how we are going to tackle a challenging situation or relationship that we become trapped in a cycle of adverse behaviour. It can help us to reframe the event by taking a step back and looking at it from another person's shoes or perspective. It gives us more points of view than just our own and helps take the heat out of a potentially stressful situation and see a relationship in a different way. By doing this, we may identify alternative solutions for tackling the problem or a more productive way in which to respond.

Perceptual positions exercise

This exercise allows you to look at a situation from three different viewpoints: your own, the other person's and that of an objective outsider.

Step 1

Identify a challenge or situation where you need more clarity, the event may have already occurred or something that is due to take place in the future. An example might be an experience of having a difficult conversation with someone close to you.

Do this exercise standing as it helps to move to a different place in the room as you change position and step into someone else's shoes. It is important to set up three separate locations or spatial anchors before you begin.

Step 2

Take a moment to imagine the scene or conversation taking place in front of you, see yourself in the first position and the other person in the second position and then think of a third position in the room which will take the place of the objective outsider space (someone you admire who has no connection with, or involvement in the situation). It's important to change spaces while completing this exercise as it helps to break state from one person to another so you can see the situation clearly from each viewpoint.

Step 3

Imagine what it's like to be inside each different person, like trying on new clothes. Step inside yourself in first position and review the situation remembering exactly what happened, what each person said and how you felt at the time. When you feel you have gathered enough information, step back outside yourself and shake off the state.

Step 4

Then step inside the other person imagining as much detail as possible, think about how that person is standing, their hand gestures and mannerisms, what are they saying and also get a sense or knowing how they are feeling during the conversation. From this position, what do you also notice about your own behaviour, approach or manner? Once you feel you have gathered enough information from their perspective, step back outside of them and shake off the state.

Step 5

When you are ready move to the third position of the objective outsider, someone who has been listening impartially to both sides of the story. While there ask yourself, how are these two people acting? Are they being fair to each other? What advice would you give to help them work out their differences? What would you do in this situation?

Take a few minutes to write down what you have learned from this exercise. What you learned about yourself and your reaction. What you learned about the other person. Think about how you want to move forward from here.

> *"I have found if you love life, life will love you back."*
> **Arthur Rubinstein**

Changing your emotional state

Our experience of the world is acquired through the data gathered by our five senses (sight, sound, taste, smell and touch), our brain then interprets that data and this becomes our internal representation. So ultimately, the experience we have and remember of something is how we have represented it internally.

Using the following technique, we can change the way we feel at any time and in any situation. This includes our feelings about a past experience, an anticipated future challenge or something occurring in the moment. We can change the feelings and level of intensity of an experience by altering the blueprint that we have of that experience.

Sit in a comfortable chair with your feet on the ground. Start to feel yourself relaxing and allow the chair to support your body. Close your eyes as you continue to relax.

Using a visual representation

Step 1

Think of an experience where you were really happy, excited or calm, or the desired positive state that you would like to get to in this exercise. Replay that memory in your head and notice what the picture of that experience is like, is it in colour or black and white? Is it bright or dark, high contrast or low contrast? Is the image sharp or fuzzy? How big is the image, is it close or at a distance? What shape is the picture, square, round or rectangular? Is there a border to the image? Is it a movie or a still picture? Do you see yourself as if you were there? Are the sizes of the things in the image in proportion to one another? Are they larger or smaller than life? Is the image 3D or flat?

Step 2

Once you have recorded all of these, turn your attention to a challenging situation you would like to change your blueprint and state for. Replay that experience or future experience in your head, what is the picture like for this one and go through the questions again. Notice what the picture of that experience is like; is it in colour or black and white? Is it bright or dark, high contrast or low contrast? Is the image sharp or fuzzy? How big is the image, is it close or at a distance? What shape is the picture, square, round or rectangular? Is there a border to the image? Is it a movie or a still picture? Do you see yourself as if you were there? Are the sizes of the things in the image in proportion to one another? Are they larger or smaller than life? Is the image 3D or flat?

Step 3

Once you have a visual representation for both, move your attention to the challenging situation again and as you do so start to change the image in alignment to the blueprint you had for your happy experience. If your happy image was in full colour make your challenging image full colour, if it was bright and a moving image, again do the same and so on until the challenging experience starts to transform into a happy image and a change in your state.

Observe the challenging situation again from your more positive state, how has this transformed the experience, what is now happening in the scene?

Using an auditory representation

Step 1

Think of an experience where you were really happy, excited or calm, or the desired positive state that you would like to get to in this exercise. Replay that memory in your head, imagine if it were a piece of music what type of music it would be, where does the sound originate, do you hear it from inside or outside? Is it high or low-pitched? Is the tempo fast or slow? Is it loud or soft, clear or muffled? Is the melody monotone or melodic? What's the beat like? Do you hear it on one side or both sides?

Step 2

Once you have recorded all of these, turn your attention to a challenging situation you would like to change your blueprint and state for. Replay that experience or future experience in your head and once again go through the questions. If it were a piece of music what type of music it would be where does the sound originate, do you hear it from inside or outside? Is it high or low-pitched? Is the tempo fast or slow? Is it loud or soft, clear or muffled? Is the melody monotone or melodic? What's the beat like? Do you hear it on one side or both sides?

Step 3

Once you have an auditory representation for both, move your attention to the challenging situation again and as you do so start to change the music in alignment to the blueprint you had for your happy experience. If your happy music's tempo was fast increase the tempo of your challenging piece of music, if it had a strong beat and was melodic, again do the same until the challenging experience starts to transform into your happy music and a change in your state.

Observe the challenging situation again from your more positive state, how has this transformed the experience, what is now happening in the scene?

Using a kinaesthetic (feeling) representation

Step 1

Think of an experience where you were really happy, excited or calm, or the desired positive state that you would like to get to in this exercise. Replay that memory, how strong is the sensation you were feeling at the time, how would you describe it? Tingling, warm, relaxed, calm? Where do you feel it in your body? Is there movement in the sensation? Is the movement continuous or does it come in waves? Does it have a temperature, hot or cold? Is the intensity strong or weak? Where does the sensation start? Where does it move to? In what direction does it move? Is it a slow progression or does it move in a rush?

Step 2

Once you have recorded all of these, turn your attention to a challenging situation you would like to change your blueprint and state for. Replay that experience or future experience in your head and once again go through the questions. How strong is the sensation you were feeling at the time, how would you describe it? Tingling, warm, relaxed, calm? Where do you feel it in your body? Is there movement in the sensation? Is the movement continuous or does it come in waves? Does it have a temperature, hot or cold? Is the intensity strong or weak? Where does the sensation start? Where does it move to? In what direction does it move? Is it a slow progression or does it move in a rush?

Step 3

Once you have kinaesthetic representation for both, move your attention to the challenging situation again and as you do so start to change the kinaesthetic representation in alignment to the blueprint you had for your happy experience. If your happy experience was a strong sensation you felt in your body that was warm and intense again do the same until the challenging experience starts to transform into your happy feeling and a change in your state.

Observe the challenging situation again from your more positive state, how has this transformed the experience, what is now happening in the scene?

You can use any of the above exercises at any time, if you find yourself faced with a challenging situation that is stressful to you, see the situation in terms of a visual, auditory or feeling representation and start to change the blueprint (picture, music or sensation), to quickly get you back into a positive state so you can face the challenge from a more productive place.

> *"Authenticity is a collection of choices that we have to make every day. It's about the choice to show up and be real. The choice to be honest. The choice to let our true selves be seen."*
>
> **Brené Brown**

Our conflicting parts

Emotional experiences, particularly during our younger years can create disconnected parts in us that we are not aware of. When we have behaviour that is conflicting, or mixed emotions about doing something or being a certain way; it is often because we have parts in us that are opposed, so 'part of us wants to stop doing something, but part of us wants to keep doing it'.

Sometimes we meet people who push our buttons or irritate us with their behaviour and we can't put our finger on why that is. Often the behaviour we dislike so much may be behaviour that we had to suppress growing up in order to please our caregivers. So if we see someone being playful or stupid and having fun - we might view it as annoying because we may have been restricted from being loud and playful as a child.

Some examples of our conflicting parts might be:

'Part of me wants security and part of me wants freedom'. In this instance we may shy away from commitment so we can be free, but then the other part pops up and wants security, so we get into a relationship and start to settle down. The part that wants freedom then rears up and we end up sabotaging or wanting out of our relationship so we can have our freedom again and the spiral continues.

Other examples might be 'part of me believes I deserve success and part of me doesn't', 'part of me trusts my decisions and part of me doesn't.

The following exercise helps to create harmony between these parts so they are more in alignment. If we become unified internally, we live more empowered lives and become clearer in our decisions and actions.

Parts integration exercise

Step 1

Think about a behaviour, bad habit or indecision that you want to change and identify at least two opposing parts to start with – let's call them the positive and negative parts or the part that wants to change and the part that keeps creating the behaviour.

All our parts whether we see them as positive or negative will have their own values and beliefs and positive intention behind the behaviour they are creating. We will always find that both parts even though they are opposites, have the same highest intention for us – maybe we want freedom to meet our need for peace which would also be the intention of the part that wants security.

Step 2

Create an image or object for both parts and hold one in each hand. You can visualise them or get a sense about them, however you want to, any symbol, image or object that springs to mind. See what each object or image looks like, sounds like and what feelings and thoughts each one has.

Step 3

Focus on each part in turn and ask the first one what its intention is for you in doing what it is doing, you will get an answer pop into your head, just go with it, then keep repeating that question on whatever answer you get each time, until you arrive at a positive value like love, freedom, joy, peace etc. Once you have reached its highest intention for you, do the same with the other part. Notice that what both parts want, their highest intention, is either the same or compatible.

Step 4

Ask each part individually what resources they have that would benefit the other part in achieving their highest intention and the shared goal of helping you. Is there anything useful about part one that will help the other part? And vice versa? Imagine both parts now sharing these positive resources and the benefits to you.

Step 5

Turn your hands towards each other and see the two images or objects begin to merge as you move your hands closer together. As your hands come together a third image or object is created that symbolises the integration of the two former parts.

Step 6

Bring this new image or object into your body by placing your hands on your heart and feeling yourself breathing it in and absorbing this new united part.

Step 7

Focus again on the old inner conflict or behaviour that you want to change, now that the conflicting parts are joined as one. Consider how you are going to approach your situation differently in the future now that you are integrated.

If there is still any doubt that you feel able to sustain the change, there may be another part that wants to speak up on the matter. If this is the case you would simply repeat this process with the newly created integrated part and the part that now wants a say, until all parts are united and playing for the same team.

"Though no one can go back and make a brand new start, anyone can start from now and make a brand new ending."

Carl Bard

Balancing our lives – Exercise and diet

It is well known that regular exercise is good for our physical health; recent studies have shown that physical activity also has benefits for our mental health. Any type of exercise can be beneficial as long as it is something that we enjoy.

When we are feeling down, exercise often seems like the last thing that we want to do but the psychological and physical benefits of exercise can help to reduce anxiety and improve mood by releasing feel-good brain chemicals.

Exercise can help you to gain confidence by meeting exercise goals or challenges that can boost self-confidence. It can take your mind off worries and provide more social interaction if it is group training. It doesn't have to be strenuous physical exercise either, regular walking, gardening or even washing the car can help to improve our mood. We are also increasing our sense of control and self-esteem by taking an active role in shifting our state.

Healthy eating is not about depriving ourselves of the foods we love or having strict dietary limitations, everything in moderation is the key. Eating a balanced diet can help to maintain a healthy weight and avoid certain health problems, but it can also have a profound effect on our mood and sense of well-being.

Prepare more of your own meals, replace packaged and processed foods with healthy alternatives using more fresh ingredients, consume more fruit and vegetables and drink plenty of water. Eat mindfully and set aside time to have meals away from watching TV or browsing your phone or computer.

"If you are brave enough to leave behind everything familiar and comforting, which can be anything from your house to your bitter, old resentments, and set out on a truth-seeking journey, either externally or internally, and if you are truly willing to regard everything that happens to you on that journey as a clue, and if you accept everyone you meet along the way as a teacher, and if you are prepared, most of all, to face and forgive some very difficult realities about yourself, then the truth will not be withheld from you."

Elizabeth Gilbert

I hope you find the colouring illustrations and mindfulness exercises useful in lots of ways and they help to create focus, balance and inner peace.

If you are still finding life a bit of a struggle, I would advise you to seek help. Whether it's with a family member, a friend, a support group, a coach, counsellor or a therapist. It does help to talk and get support from other people. To me, rather than it being a weakness, admitting we need some help is a huge strength. We are saying to ourselves that we are not prepared to accept life as it is any more and are ready to face our issues head-on. We all deserve to be happy in life; we just need to believe ourselves worthy of happiness.

You deserve to be happy, believe that and take some action today!

Lots of love,
Tracy. x

Find out more at www.tracybadau.com or search on Facebook for 'Reflections: An Exploration of Self'

Resources

Books

The Power of Now, Eckhart Tolle, Hachette, 2004

A New Earth, Eckhart Tolle, Penguin Group, 2005

A Thousand Names for Joy, Byron Katie, Rider, 2007

Who Would You Be Without Your Story? Byron Katie, Hay House, 2008

The Astonishing Power of Emotions, Esther and Jerry Hicks, Hay House, 2007

The Vortex, Esther and Jerry Hicks, Hay House, 2009

Daring Greatly, Brene Brown, Penguin Group, 2012

The Diamond in your Pocket, Gangaji, Sounds Ture, Inc., Boulder, CO 2007

You are the Placebo, Dr Joe Dispenza, Hay House, 2014

Excuse me your life is waiting, Lynn Grabhorn, Hampton Roads, 2005

Courage, Osho, Osho International Foundation, 1999

The Artist's Way, Julia Cameron, Pan Books, 1995

Messages from Water, Masaru Emoto, HAO Kyoikusha, Tokyo, 2000

Emotional Intelligence, Daniel Goleman, Bantam Books, New York 1995

The Art of Happiness, HH Dalai Lama & Howard C. Cutler, Tans. Dr. Thupten Jinpa. Riverhead Books, New York 1998

The Journey, Brandon Bays, Astria Paperback, 1999

Zero Limits, Dr. Joe Vitale and Dr. Ihaleakala Hew Len, PH.D, John Wiley & Sons, 2007

Metaphors in Mind, James Lawley & Penny Tompkins, The Developing Company, 2000

Get off your 'Butt', Sean Stephenson, Wiley, 2009

Videos

What the Bleep!? – Down the Rabbit Hole, (Quantum Three-Disc Special Edition) 2013

Zero Limits III The Final Chapter, Live from Austin, Tx, 2 Day Seminar on DVD

Courses

NLP Training, Inspiritive, www.inspiritive.com.au

Strategic Intervention and Coach Training, Robbins Madanes Training, www.rmtcenter.com

Clean Language Training, James Lawley and Penny Tompkins, www.cleanlanguage.co.uk

Unlimited Abundance, Christie Marie Sheldon, www.mindvalley.com

Love or Above, Christie Marie Sheldon, www.mindvalley.com

Duality Energy Training, Jeffrey Allen, www.mindvalley.com